dabblelab

PROJECT PASSION

Create and KEEP

Projects to Hang on To

by Mari Bolte

CAPSTONE PRESS
a capstone imprint

Dabble Lab is published by Capstone Press,
1710 Roe Crest Drive, North Mankato, Minnesota 56003
www.mycapstone.com

Library of Congress Cataloging-in-Publication Data is available
on the Library of Congress website.

ISBN: 978-1-5157-7373-3 (library hardover)
ISBN: 978-1-5157-7377-1 (eBook PDF)

Editorial Credits:
Kayla Rossow, designer; Tori Abraham, production specialist

Photo Credits:
All photos by Capstone Studio/Karon Dubke
Background design elements by Shutterstock
Project production by Marcy Morin, Kayla Rossow, Mari Bolte,
and Sarah Schuette

Printed in Canada.
010395F17

Table of Contents

A weekend of crafting is a great way to
spend some time by yourself or with friends.
But when the weekend is over, are you left
with a pile of projects you'll throw away later,
or will you have projects you want to keep?
Turn your passion into projects that will stay
with you no matter where you go.

Found Fun

Use old objects found around the house to create signs and messages with bits of history already built in.

How to:

Old pieces of scrap wood make great backdrops for found metal decorations. If you don't have scrap wood, you can find distressed wood at craft stores.

Pick out hardware pieces to create letters. Have an adult use heavy-duty pliers to bend nails or other metal pieces, if necessary. Attach metal to the wood with hot glue. Let the glue dry completely before displaying your artwork.

Variation:

• Wrap metal pieces with contrasting wire. Experiment with wire gauges and twist tightness. Add beads if desired, or use leather cording instead.

Tip: Heavier pieces may need a stronger glue, such as a metal epoxy. Have an adult help with epoxy.

Variations:

• Add accent pieces, such as faux flowers, moss, bits of leather, or rustic fabric.

• Glue a large metal letter onto your wood. Use smaller letters or numbers to spell out a name. You could also use small numbers to add your house number over a large letter. Another option is to attach a decorative key — or a key that has special meaning to you.

♥ TRY IT!

Tip: You can find letters made of metal or corrugated metal in craft stores and online.

♥ TRY IT!

Variations:

• Attach nuts or washers with jump rings to make a chain. Use the chain to spell out letters on your sign, or use it to frame your piece of wood. Use different kinds of nuts or washers to mix up the look and change the size.

• Add a lobster clasp to one end of your chain to turn it into a heavy-duty bracelet or necklace.

7

Sweet Stitches

Update embroidery thread with a modern twist—pair it with bright designs or coloring pages! The hours you spend coloring to de-stress will finally be on display for others to admire.

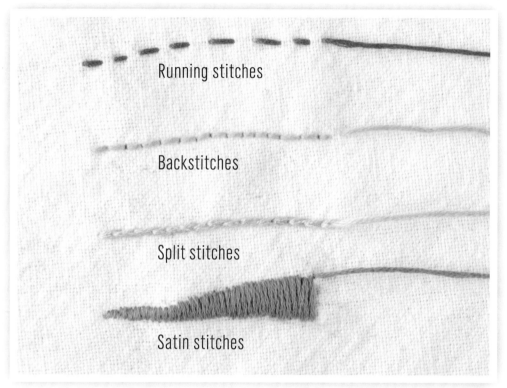

Running stitches

Backstitches

Split stitches

Satin stitches

Cross-stitch is a fun and easy activity! Start with the simplest stitches before you get started.

Running stitches are the most basic. Just push the needle and thread in and out of the fabric. Use a running stitch to outline designs.

Backstitches are similar to running stitches. Pull the needle and thread up through the fabric and the back down to create a stitch. Make a stitch on the underside of the fabric and push the needle and thread up through the fabric.

Loop the thread back through the hole of the previous stitch. Backstitches are good for creating solid lines.

Split stitches use a similar technique to backstitches. Make a stitch, and then push the needle and thread up through the middle of the previous stitch before making another full stitch. This makes thicker solid lines.

Satin stitches are simply a series or block of stitches that line up close together. Use satin stitches to color in areas of your pattern.

1. Choose a design that will fit inside an embroidery hoop. Tape a coloring page onto a window. Place a piece of linen over the coloring page, and use a pencil to trace the design. Center the linen in the embroidery hoop, and close the rings. The fabric should be taught so it makes a slight noise like a drum when tapped.

2. Now you can start stitching! Use running or back stitches for outlines. Color in bare spaces with satin or split stitches.

3. When you're done embroidering, remove your fabric and display it in a frame.

Variation:

You can also embroider on paper! Use thick paper to avoid tearing. Stitch the edges, and then use crayons or markers to color in your design.

♥ TRY IT!

♥ TRY IT!

Jeweled Jars

Color mason jars or glass bottles with a quick coat of paint. Use them to store extra craft supplies, or show off your green thumb.

How to:

Gently wash your jar, and then rub a cotton ball dipped in rubbing alcohol over the entire jar. Paint the outside of the jar with chalkboard paint. Let dry, and then add a second layer.

If you want a vintage look, gently rub sandpaper over your paint job.

Variation:

• For a shinier finish, paint the inside of the jars instead. Pour 2 to 3 ounces (29.6 to 59 milliliters) of acrylic paint into your jar. Then tilt the jar until the entire inside is coated. Set the jar upside-down on a well-covered work surface and let the excess paint drip out.

After 15 to 20 minutes, rotate the jar again. Repeat two to three more times. Then let the jar sit upside-down until the paint is completely dry.

Variations:

Paint on small details with a fine brush. Ideas include:

- flowers
- bugs
- stripes and polka dots
- snowflakes
- patterns, such as animal prints or chevron designs
- emoji faces

Tip: You can also use enamel, glitter paint, and spray paint. Dry times may vary, and spray paint will require a well-protected outdoor work surface.

♥ TRY IT!

Variation:

- Forget gift wrap — use your jars instead! Give people a window into what's inside by leaving an unpainted space. Press on a large sticker or vinyl shape before painting. When the paint is dry, remove the sticker. Paint the jar's lid in a contrasting color, if you want.

♥ TRY IT!

Bursts of Color

Use washi or painter's tape to make a wall hanging to catch the eye.
This painted project will be a statement piece in whatever room you display it.

Steps:

1. Choose two or more pieces of wood paneling. Use washi or painter's tape to block out a design over the wood. The designs should work together and coordinate across the pieces of wood.

2. Use a sponge to apply acrylic paint over the wood. Let the paint dry completely before peeling off the tape.

3. Attach hardware to hang your wood pieces on the wall.

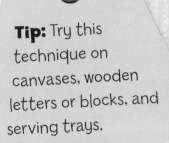

Tip: Try this technique on canvases, wooden letters or blocks, and serving trays.

Variations:

• Try spray paint instead. Have an adult help you spray a variety of colors onto the wood. Use short bursts for more concentrated spots of color.

• Use many small pieces of wood. Paint each a different color, or create a rainbow or gradient effect that will stretch across your wall.

• Try this technique on a drinking glass (or even a mason jar). Have an adult spray the outside with an acrylic sealer to help the paint last through washings.

• Use stickers or vinyl instead of tape. Peel the stickers or vinyl away. Tape a string of lights to the back of the canvas, and then plug them in for backlit art.

• Puffy paint can add some 3D fun to your canvas. Outline all the painted edges with black puffy paint. Or use similar-colored puffy paint to add swirls or dotted patterns over the color blocks.

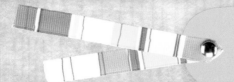

Tip: Overlap short pieces of tape to create curves and bends in your lines.

13

Shimmering Shells

There's no reason plastic eggs should get the once-a-year treatment. Display decorated eggs year-round after some amazing alterations.

Steps:

1. Gold is old-school. Glitter is the way to go! Use fine sanding paper to lightly sand the outside of an egg.

2. Paint the egg with decoupage glue, and sprinkle with glitter. Let the glue dry. Then add another glue coat. Use more glitter to cover any bare spots.

3. Continue gluing and glittering until the entire egg is covered. One final layer of glue will keep the glitter from shedding.

Variations:

• Give your eggs an extra level of awesome with 3D designs. Use a hot glue gun or puffy paint to pipe a design onto the egg. Give the egg an all-over coat of paint afterward, if desired.

• If you're not into glitter, paint will have a similar effect. Sand the egg and then paint it with primer. Once the primer is dry, brush on your favorite colors of paint. Permanent markers can be used to create geometric shapes across the surface of the egg.

Shell-y Soap

Simple soaps that fit perfectly in the palm of your hand?
Nothing could be easier to make – or give as a gift.

Tip: The plastic eggs also make natural gift packaging. Use them as molds, and then decorate the outside to match your gift-giving occasion. Place the finished soap inside.

Steps:

1. Have an adult use a small drill to make a hole at the top of an egg. Open the egg and add a pinch of glitter or sprinkles to the inside. Close the egg and use electric tape to seal it shut.

2. With an adult's help, cut melt and pour soap into ½ inch (1.3 cm) cubes. Place the cubes in a microwave-safe dish and heat for 30 seconds. Stir. Continue heating and stirring until the soap is completely melted. Then stir in body-safe soap fragrance or essential oils.

3. Use a piece of parchment paper to make a funnel, and place it through the hole in the egg. Have an adult slowly pour the soap into the egg. When the egg is full, set it on a stable surface and let the soap harden before removing it from the mold.

Tip: If your soap egg has a line around the middle from where the egg halves met, don't worry! Just smooth it down with your fingers, or have a grown-up remove the excess with a craft knife.

Halves or Wholes

Everyone outgrows their toys. But don't be so quick to get rid of old favorites! Keep them around a little while longer with these zoo-themed projects.

Steps:

1. Have an adult cut a plastic animal in half. If your animal is hollow, have an adult help you fill the space with resin or expanding foam. Cut off any excess fill, and file the rough edges down with a nail file or sandpaper. Give the pieces a quick wash with warm, soapy water. Let them dry.

2. Paint the animals, if desired. Spray paint or craft paint made specifically for painting on plastic will work best. Add a magnet on each cut end for some in-your-face fridge décor or some stand-alone sign holders.

Tip: Box cutters or small saw blades work well for cutting animals in half. This is an adult-only part of the project! Let them help with the spray paint too.

♥ TRY IT!

Variations:

- Attach suction cups instead of magnets.

- Glue two wood blocks together at a right angle. Attach an animal half to one block. Paint the entire thing with spray paint. Repeat with a second pair of blocks. Now you have some wild bookends!

- How about a bookmark that will ensure you'll never lose your spot? Have an adult saw a slit about ¼-inch (0.6-cm)-long across the bottom of a small animal. Insert a paper or plastic bookmark into the slit, and glue it in place.

♥ TRY IT!

Delicious Outdoors

Make a plain birdhouse extra inviting with a delicious outside.
Your backyard will never be so wild!

For the Birdhouse:

1 ¼ cup (300 milliliters)
   whole-wheat flour
½ cup (120 mL) oats
½ cup cornmeal
½ cup butter, melted
½ teaspoon (2.5 mL)
   baking powder
2 eggs, whole
1 cup (240 mL) dried
   fruit or vegetables
1 cup birdseed

Steps:

1. Trace the roof and sides of the birdhouse onto paper. Cut out the pieces, and set aside. There's no need to trace smaller parts, such as ledges or perches.

2. Mix the flour, oats, cornmeal, butter, baking powder, and eggs until well combined. Make sure the eggshells are well crushed.

3. Add the dried fruit or vegetables and birdseed. Stir well.

4. Turn the birdseed dough onto a clean work surface, and roll until about ½ inch (1.3 cm) thick. Sprinkle additional birdseed onto the dough for decoration, if desired. Place the template for the birdhouse onto the dough. Have an adult help you cut out each piece.

5. Place the pieces onto a baking sheet lined with parchment paper. Bake for 15 minutes at 325 degrees Fahrenheit (160 degrees Celsius) until firm. Let cool completely.

For the Glue:

1 package unflavored gelatin
½ cup water
3 tablespoons (45 mL) honey
¾ cup (175 mL) whole-wheat flour

Steps:

1. Dissolve the gelatin in the water. Then add the remaining ingredients. Mix well.

2. Use the glue to attach the birdseed pieces to the birdhouse. Use the edible glue to decorate perches, chimneys, and other exterior decorations your birdhouse may have. Let the birdhouse dry completely before placing outside.

Sharing Is Caring

Share your snacks in a super stylish way! These quick DIY snack bags are reusable, so fill them over and over again.

Steps:

1. Cut a piece of fabric 5 by 12 inches (12.7 by 30.5 cm). Have an adult cut a piece of lightweight vinyl to the same measurements. Place the pieces togther with the wrong sides touching, and pin the edges. Sew along the two long sides and one short side. Then flip the pieces right-side-out.

Steps:

2. Sew the open edge shut. Then fold the vinyl side in, leaving about 1 ½ inches (3.8 cm) near the top of the bag for the flap. Sew the edges together where they meet. Glue or sew hook and loop fasteners to the bag, to close the flap.

Tip: A rotary cutter will make a quick job of cutting through fabric and vinyl.

Tip: Vinyl isn't necessary, but it will help keep your food fresh. For an easier — but less durable — bag, cut pieces from a disposable plastic tablecloth.

♥ TRY IT!

Variations:

• Instead of hook-and-loop fasteners, sew a button onto the bag. Add a piece of elastic or ribbon to the top flap to close.

• Sew on a long piece of ribbon to make a mini carrying bag.

• Make bags of any size! Increase the size to hold sandwiches, or create a tiny bag for a single cookie.

• Add a name or a label. Use iron-on letters before sewing the fabric and vinyl together.

Light-Up Lanterns

Light the way with lanterns! Use a battery-operated tea light and a tea light holder – large or small – to ensure your projects shine bright.

Steps:

1. Select a piece of paper large enough to fit around a tea light and tea light holder. Trim the paper if necessary.

2. Select a photo to trace. Images with thick, clear lines work best. Place the paper over the photo, and trace the photo's outlines with a pencil. The tracings should stretch from edge to edge on the paper. If the tracings don't stretch that far, just reposition the paper and duplicate the photo to fill the blank space.

3. When the tracing is to your liking, use a black permanent marker to re-trace the pencil lines.

4. Roll the paper into a tube and tape the edges together. Then set the paper tube over the tea light holder.

♥ TRY IT!

Variations:

- Instead of using a permanent marker on the outlines, use a thin needle. Poke evenly spaced holes along the pencil tracings. The light will shine through the holes.

- Tape your image on a paper lampshade. Use the pin technique to outline the image's design. Remove the image, and place the lampshade on a lamp.

- Instead of tracing a whole image, use a large hole punch to remove shapes around your lamp paper. Accentuate the punched holes with small pinholes.

Tip: Vary the distance between pinholes. Light will be more intense when the pinholes are closer together.

A Sporting Challenge

Show everyone you're the biggest fan with a sports-specific message board! Customize it to fit the sport you love best.

Steps:

1. To make a softball board, paint a round cork board fluorescent yellow. Let the paint dry completely, and add a second coat, if desired.

2. Use red paint to add curved lines in two of the corners. Use short lines to paint laces on the "ball." When the red paint is dry, glue chipboard numbers onto the cork board.

Variations:

• Paint on your number using your team colors and number stencils.

• Turn the softball board into a baseball board with a quick color change. Use white paint instead of fluorescent yellow.

Hockey Shot

Steps:

1. To make a hockey board, use a combo cork board and magnetic white board. Decorate the cork board with a hockey stick and puck done with acrylic paint.

2. Use red and blue hockey tape to make rink lines on the white board.

3. Paint the rink circles with red paint. Let the paint dry before using your board.

Variation:

• Glue each player's photo or number onto small, disc-shaped magnets. Paint one magnet black, for the puck. Use the magnets to hang sports schedules, player's cards or autographs, and team photos. Keep the unused magnets in the score boxes.

Tip: A compass or appropriately-sized round object (such as a glass or can) will help with the rink circles.

Soccer Stats

Steps:

1. Turn a clipboard into a soccer board! Cover the metal clip with newspaper to protect it. Then paint the rest of the board with chalkboard paint. Let the paint dry completely, and add a second coat, if desired.

2. Use a white chalk marker to draw a soccer ball in the corner of the board, or use a sticker or vinyl soccer ball.

3. Use chalk, or chalk markers, to plan your team's next play.

Variations:

• Decorate the bottom inch or two of the clipboard with a strip of artificial turf instead of a soccer ball sticker.

• For a football board, paint the clipboard with brown chalkboard paint. Add laces from corner to corner, if desired.

B-ball Board

1. Turn an old photo frame into a slam dunk dry erase board. Take the frame apart and set the backing aside. Paint the frame orange. Use a fine-tipped paintbrush and a darker shade of orange or brown to add texture similar to a basketball's.

2. Cut a piece of white heavy-duty cardstock to fit inside your frame. Use a marker to color the edge of the cardstock black. Draw a smaller rectangle near the bottom of the cardstock, to resemble a backboard. Reassemble the frame. You can draw directly on the frame's glass with a dry erase marker.

3. Wrap a long piece of yarn around a large orange puffball. Tie the other end of the yarn to the frame's edge. Use the puffball as mini basketball — or a dry erase eraser.

Variations:

• Instead of drawing the backboard, print your team's logo onto the cardstock.

• Get really playful and add a large binder ring to the bottom of the frame to make a hoop. Use red yarn to weave a net.

Millions of Meltys

Fusion beads are fun and come in dozens of colors.
Make fabulous fused projects for each of your friends
(and keep one in each color for yourself!)

1. Use a large pegboard to create a modern vintage frame. The edges should be 5 inches (12.7 cm) square. Use two or three layers of white beads around the edge, or add a few extra layers along the bottom for a vintage look.

2. Make a second square, but fill in all the edges. Iron the square. Once the square is cooled, glue beads along three of the edges. Then glue the frame to the square. The added beads will make it easy to slide images in and out of the frame.

3. Attach magnets to the back of the square for an easy-to-display frame. Slide images in and out for an ever-changing slideshow.

Variations:

Add colors and patterns to your frame instead of using just white! You can also vary the size to fit standard 4 by 6 inch (10.2 by 15.2 cm) or 5 by 7 inch (12.7 by 17.8 cm) photos. Try making smaller frames to fit your friends' school pictures!

Fusion Bead Tips: Have an adult read this before starting! It will make their (and your) life much easier.

Use a preheated iron on low to medium-low heat. Iron your pieces out on a flat surface. If your surface is fabric-covered (such as a tablecloth), iron the work surface too.

Iron in a slow, circular motion, and press slightly. Small pieces should get about 20 seconds of heat; large pieces can take up to 45-50 seconds.

Keep your pegboard safe. Instead of ironing right on the board, cover your finished design with strips of masking tape. Make sure each strip overlaps slightly. Remove any excess tape. Then carefully flip your design over. Carefully remove the pegboard, and iron directly over the beads. Let the beads cool. Flip the design over and remove the tape. Gently iron this side too.

overmelted beads

melted beads

Beady Bracelet

How to:

Turn your beads into jewelry! Set beads hole-side-up on a baking sheet lined with parchment paper. Preheat your oven to 400 degrees F (200 degrees C). Let the beads bake in the oven for 5 minutes. When the beads are flat, have an adult remove them from the oven, and let them cool. You can use the melted beads as you would any other type of bead.

Stitch Inspired

How to:

Never run out of ideas! Look online for cross-stitch or quilting patterns. The style is similar to fusion beads, and there are many more project plans out there. Be sure to account for the fact that beads are much larger than stitches — you may end up with big finished projects!

Variations:

Try an inside-out pattern. Leave a blank space in the center, and build beads around that space. Hang your finished piece to show off your design.

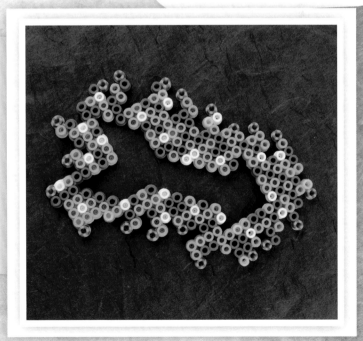

Read More

Ceceri, Kathy. *Paper Inventions: Machines that Move, Drawings that Light Up, and Wearables and Structures You Can Cut, Fold, and Roll.* San Francisco: Maker Media, 2015.

Uliana, Kim. *Crafting Fun for Kids of All Ages: Pipe Cleaners, Paint & Pom-Poms Galore, Yarn & String & a Whole Lot More.* New York: Sky Pony Press, 2017.

Ventura, Marne. *A Girls Guide to the Perfect Sleepover.* North Mankato, Mlnn.: Capstone Press, 2017.

Internet Sites

Use FactHound to find Internet sites related to this book.

Visit *www.facthound.com*

Just type in 9781515773733 and go!

 Check out projects, games and lots more at
www.capstonekids.com

Maker Space Tips

Download tips and tricks for using this book and others in a library maker space.

Visit *www.capstonepub.com/dabblelabresources*